MOTIVATED
TO
ACTIVATED

7 STEPS TO SUCCESS, JOY
AND INNER PEACE

BRIDGET L CHARLES

ISBN-10: 0-692-59784-0
ISBN-13: 978-0-692-59784-2
Printed in the United States of America

MOTIVATED TO ACTIVATED

DEDICATION

This book is dedicated to my daughter, Taylor, my ultimate reason why I strive to continue to be the best me that I can be.

To my husband, Tony, the love of my life and my best friend. I could not imagine embarking upon this journey called life with anyone else.

To the greatest mother in the world, Juritta. The person who has given me strength and confidence and helped me to become the person that I am today.

To my sisters (entirely too many to name), extended family, friends and audience; your support means more to me than you could ever imagine.

BRIDGET L CHARLES

MOTIVATED TO ACTIVATED

CONTENTS

BRIDGET L CHARLES

ACKNOWLEDGMENTS

To the Empower Many Team - for your countless hours on this project to make this material available to everyone across this great world.

To those who realize that motivation alone is not enough and that taking action is a requirement to reaching your dreams.

To those seeking a more abundant life all across the world and to those who have had the courage to seek what is rightfully theirs and to do it boldly!

FOREWORD

Bridget has hit the ball out of the park by carefully explaining the steps to success. I often find myself apologizing for seeking a more abundant life. Not merely from an inner peace or joyous standpoint but definitely from a monetary perspective. This book allowed me to see that it is possible to maintain your faith while seeking success. It allowed me to see that when I prosper, I have the ability to help more people. It has also shown me that you are never too old to dream, to find your life's purpose, all while maintaining a renowned sense of inner peace and joy. Bridget proves that you can have your cake and eat it too, of course, as long as you are sharing it with others.

~ Demishia Wright,

The Corporate Entrepreneur

"EVERYONE HAS A SUCCESS MECHANISM
AND A FAILURE MECHANISM. THE FAILURE
MECHANISM GOES OFF BY ITSELF. THE
SUCCESS MECHANISM ONLY GOES OFF WITH
A GOAL. EVERY TIME WE WRITE DOWN AND
TALK ABOUT A GOAL WE PUSH THE
BUTTON TO START THE SUCCESS
MECHANISM".
- CHARLES 'TREMENDOUS' JONES

"THE GREATEST AMOUNT OF WASTED TIME
IS THE TIME NOT GETTING STARTED."
- DAWSON TROTMAN

"IF YOUR DREAMS DO NOT SCARE YOU,
THEY ARE NOT BIG ENOUGH."
- ELLEN JOHNSON SIRLEAF

The Art of Defining Success

BRIDGET L CHARLES

"THE REAL OPPORTUNITY FOR SUCCESS LIES WITHIN THE PERSON AND NOT IN THE JOB." - ZIG ZIGLAR

Let us begin by cutting to the chase, everyone ultimately wants to be successful. However, it is important to understand that everyone defines success differently.

Some people define success in terms of how much money they make, how much money is in their bank account or what titles they hold in their chosen career.

Others define success as waking up every day, getting dress and going to a job or doing something that they absolutely love to do.

"SUCCESSFUL AND UNSUCCESSFUL PEOPLE DO NOT VARY GREATLY IN THEIR ABILITIES. THEY VARY IN THEIR DESIRES TO REACH THEIR POTENTIAL."
- JOHN MAXWELL

The communal textbook definition of success is a person who achieves desired aims or attains prosperity.

Regardless, as to how you define success it is important to remember that success does not provide that feeling of euphoria without inner peace and joy.

Your next question may be, "Is it really possible to have it all? Success, joy and inner peace?"

"SUCCESS? I DON'T KNOW WHAT THAT WORD MEANS. I'M HAPPY. BUT SUCCESS, THAT GOES BACK TO WHAT IN SOMEBODY'S EYES SUCCESS MEANS. FOR ME, SUCCESS IS INNER PEACE. THAT'S A GOOD DAY FOR ME." - DENZEL WASHINGTON

The answer to that questions without a moment of hesitation is ABSOLUTELY yes, yes and yes!

Join me on this journey as I share seven steps to assist you in reaching your goal of being successful and happy while basking in total inner peace.

"IF YOU REALLY BELIEVE IN WHAT YOU'RE DOING, WORK HARD, TAKE NOTHING PERSONALLY AND IF SOMETHING BLOCKS ONE ROUTE, FIND ANOTHER. NEVER GIVE UP." - LAURIE NOTARO

Step # 1

Self-Reflection

"A LITTLE REFLECTION WILL SHOW US
THAT EVERY BELIEF, EVEN THE SIMPLEST
AND MOST FUNDAMENTAL, GOES BEYOND
EXPERIENCE WHEN REGARDED AS A GUIDE
TO OUR ACTIONS."
- WILLIAM KINGDON CLIFFORD

The very first step to finding your calling in life is self-reflection.

Self-reflection in terms of going to a quiet place and thinking back to a time in your life when you were totally happy. Happy to the point of it being contagious and you not being able to hide or suppress your happiness.

Now, think back to the place and stage that you were in during that period in your life.

"WITHOUT REFLECTION, WE GO BLINDLY ON OUR WAY, CREATING MORE UNINTENDED CONSEQUENCES, AND FAILING TO ACHIEVE ANYTHING USEFUL."
- MARGARET J. WHEATLEY

Once you are able to reflect and pinpoint that exact moment, use the note section or bonus journal in the back of this book and jot down your conclusions.

"THE SOIL IN WHICH THE MEDITATIVE MIND CAN BEGIN IS THE SOIL OF EVERYDAY LIFE, THE STRIFE, THE PAIN, AND THE FLEETING JOY. IT MUST BEGIN THERE, AND BRING ORDER, AND FROM THERE MOVE ENDLESSLY. BUT IF YOU ARE CONCERNED ONLY WITH MAKING ORDER, THEN THAT VERY ORDER WILL BRING ABOUT ITS OWN LIMITATION, AND THE MIND WILL BE ITS PRISONER. IN ALL THIS MOVEMENT YOU MUST SOMEHOW BEGIN FROM THE OTHER END, FROM THE OTHER SHORE, AND NOT ALWAYS BE CONCERNED WITH THIS SHORE OR HOW TO CROSS THE RIVER. YOU MUST TAKE A PLUNGE INTO THE WATER, NOT KNOWING HOW TO SWIM. AND THE BEAUTY OF MEDITATION IS THAT YOU NEVER KNOW WHERE YOU ARE, WHERE YOU ARE GOING, WHAT THE END IS." - JIDDU KRISHNAMURTI

No matter how trivial you think the details may be, write down every facet that comes to mind regarding that exact moment or stretch of time in your life.

Next, write down details regarding your current life and exactly how you are feeling at this precise moment. Do not attempt to 'sugar coat' any details; keep it raw, genuine and straight to the point.

"LOOK WELL INTO THYSELF; THERE IS A SOURCE OF STRENGTH WHICH WILL ALWAYS SPRING UP IF THOU WILT ALWAYS LOOK THERE."
- MARCUS AURELIUS

Next, take a moment to determine what has precisely changed from that initial account of total bliss until the present moment.

For instance - perhaps you have a challenging career, you have tremendous stress in either your personal or professional life; or perhaps both. You may have a few failed goals, failed businesses or general hardships that may have occurred over time.

"IT IS NECESSARY ... FOR A MAN TO GO AWAY BY HIMSELF ... TO SIT ON A ROCK ... AND ASK, 'WHO AM I, WHERE HAVE I BEEN, AND WHERE AM I GOING?"
- CARL SANDBURG

At this point do not attempt to think of solutions to the problems, this exercise is simply to determine where you are in life and to allow you the opportunity to be in the moment.

This exercise basically allows you the opportunity to be in tune with your feelings during this specific interval.

"DON'T QUIT. NEVER GIVE UP TRYING TO BUILD THE WORLD YOU CAN SEE, EVEN IF OTHERS CAN'T SEE IT. LISTEN TO YOUR DRUM AND YOUR DRUM ONLY. IT'S THE ONE THAT MAKES THE SWEETEST SOUND."
- SIMON SINEK

The last and final task of this step is to take twenty minutes and simply be still; be tranquil both physically and mentally.

Take this time to pray or meditate and ask for guidance on the journey that you are in the process of embarking upon.

"WHEN YOU GET INTO A TIGHT PLACE AND EVERYTHING GOES AGAINST YOU, TILL IT SEEMS AS THOUGH YOU COULD NOT HANG ON A MINUTE LONGER, NEVER GIVE UP THEN, FOR THAT IS JUST THE PLACE AND TIME THAT THE TIDE WILL TURN."
- HARRIET BEECHER STOWE

Step # 2

Declare IT

"SUCCESS BEGINS AT THAT MAGICAL
MOMENT WHEN YOU DECLARE TO
YOURSELF, YOUR FRIENDS, AND THE
UNIVERSE THAT YOU BELIEVE YOU CAN DO
SOMETHING DIFFERENT."
- NATALIE MASSENET

Every day presents a new day and a new opportunity to be rejoiceful. It allows us the opportunity to have a do-over of the previous day.

When you reflect, it allows you to think of what you could have done better or differently in your efforts to become a happier, more successful person.

It is important to begin and end each day with a moment of reflection, meditation or prayer. This allows your mind and body to be free of clutter and on one accord.

"WITH THE NEW DAY COMES NEW
STRENGTH AND NEW THOUGHTS."
- ELEANOR ROOSEVELT

Think of this exercise as the equivalent of discovering your GPS system in your vehicle. Imagine that you just discovered the built in GPS system on the dashboard of your brand new vehicle and you are not yet at the point of inputting the address to get you to your desired destination.

Before you begin drafting your roadmap, you need to perform a complete purge of your current thoughts.

"I PURGE COMPULSIVELY. I'M CONSTANTLY SHEDDING THINGS." - ANDREW SULLIVAN

In order to be successful at attaining these goals, you have to purge your mind of all negative thoughts and self-doubt. Do not stop for a moment to think of your previous failures, do not think of how close you were to success before your plans were derailed in the past.

Do not think of a long daunting list of reasons that you MAY go off course this time. It is important to remember that this reinvention will not happen overnight; it will take both time and dedication to accomplish this goal.

"MY LEGACY IS THAT I STAYED ON COURSE... FROM THE BEGINNING TO THE END, BECAUSE I BELIEVED IN SOMETHING INSIDE OF ME." - TINA TURNER

REMEMBER......Success is part action and part mindset. You have to mentally tell yourself and believe without a shadow of a doubt that you WILL be successful, happy and have inner peace. You will have to own it, live it and speak it into existence.

You will have to become your biggest cheerleader, your biggest fan and in some cases perhaps even your entire fan club.

"PRIVATE DREAMS ARE THE MOST POWERFUL. YOU HAVE TO DREAM OF SUCCESS TO MAKE IT HAPPEN, AND IF YOU DON'T BELIEVE IN YOURSELF, NOBODY ELSE WILL. BUT THAT DOESN'T MEAN YOU HAVE TO GO AROUND TELLING EVERYONE ABOUT IT." - TONY MCCOY

It is important to remember that your mind operates like a computer. Your mind can be programmed to produce specific results. You can choose to either program it with good data in the form of positive thinking or bad data in the form of negative thinking.

As tempting as it may be, it is important that you do not tell people about your dreams too soon. I know that you are probably thinking that it is okay to share it with your family, closest friends and your inner circle, correct?

"I THINK ANY TIME SOMEONE'S DREAMS ARE CRUSHED, THERE'S THE PEOPLE WHO CAN FIGHT TO STILL TRY AND FULFILL THOSE DREAMS AND THEN THERE'S THE PEOPLE WHO JUST GIVE UP."
- CONSTANCE ZIMMER

Well....let me tell you this – the people who you expect will support you, the ones who you feel will certainly be in your corner, probably will not be that supportive.

The ironic thing is that the ones you think will support you the least will oftentimes offer the most support.

At this stage I am certain that you have discovered that not only is it important to have a positive mindset yourself, it is equally important to steer clear of negative people.

"PEOPLE WANT TO SAY SOMETHING NEGATIVE BEFORE THEY SAY SOMETHING GOOD." - ESTELLE

Although it is nearly impossible to avoid people all together, during this time of transition it is important to minimize exposure to toxic people. This can be accomplished by focusing entirely on your goals and your quest to get to the next level on your journey.

If you have no other option and you must be around individuals that are negative or uninviting, simply be cordial while keeping your distance.

"WATCH OUT FOR THE JOY-STEALERS: GOSSIP, CRITICISM, COMPLAINING, FAULTFINDING, AND A NEGATIVE, JUDGMENTAL ATTITUDE." - JOYCE MEYER

Limit conversations and interactions as much as possible. This is not to say that you should appear to have chip on your shoulder or be unapproachable, this simply means that you should have limits.

Say hello and if they try to engage you, merely excuse yourself and let them know that you are super busy and cannot stick around to chat.

If you find yourself in a team setting with these type of individuals, contribute to the project, keep it professional and move on.

"THE MIND IS THE ROOT FROM WHICH ALL THINGS GROW IF YOU CAN UNDERSTAND THE MIND, EVERYTHING ELSE IS INCLUDED." – BODHIDHARMA

It is possible to participate in a joint venture on a professional level while not getting too personal. The bottom line is that you cannot give them the opportunity or the forum to impose on your space with the negativity that they offer.

I cannot emphasize how important it is to surround yourself with like-minded people. Being around like-minded people will propel you to always strive toward excellence.

"AS LONG AS YOUR DETERMINATION IS AT LEAST AS LONG AS THE ROAD YOU TRAVEL, YOU WILL DEFINITELY REACH YOUR DESTINATION!"
- MEHMET MURAT ILDAN

Remember, if you are the smartest or most driven person in your circle, then perhaps it is time to change your circle.

Just as our bodies physically grow and change over time, so does our minds. Mentally, you may be on a totally different level than most of the individuals in your current circle.

"IN THEIR WORK, THEN, AS IN THEIR PLAY, MEN AND WOMEN ARE MORE AND MORE COMING TO SHARE WITH EACH OTHER AS COMRADES, AND REALLY THE FUN OF LIFE SEEMS IN NO WISE DIMINISHED AS A CONSEQUENCE."
- RICHARD LE GALLIENNE

Grant yourself permission to reevaluate your current circle of friends and acquaintances and to begin moving by expanding your circle to include more successful people in your quest to elevate your life. After all, when you see someone living what you consider to be the life of your dreams, it puts a burning fire in your soul that propels you to take immediate action to reach your desired level of success.

You wake up thinking to yourself that you have to make up for lost time. After having a conversation with them, you receive the confirmation that you desired and you are absolutely certain that you can make it!

"I WILL KEEP SMILING, BE POSITIVE AND NEVER GIVE UP! I WILL GIVE 100 PERCENT EACH TIME I PLAY. THESE ARE ALWAYS MY GOALS AND MY ATTITUDE."
-YANI TSENG

On the contrary, if you hang around people who does not have that drive, passion and success, it grants you the opportunity to not go as hard as you should and allows you ample opportunity to make excuses and procrastinate in reaching your desired level of success.

A great platform to connect with like-minded personages include but are not limited to local meet up groups in your area, networking events, mastermind classes, webinars, seminars and industry retreats.

"ALWAYS DREAM. NEVER GIVE UP!"
- TONY OLLER

Connecting with individuals or groups that share your goals and dreams will open up doors that you could never imagine. The comradery will make you more confident and keep you motivated. You will discover that your dreams will quickly become reality.

If you are one of those people who cannot suppress the urge to share your dreams with others, then only share them with people who you are confident shares the same dreams. This is the one exception to sharing your dreams!

"EACH PERSON HOLDS SO MUCH POWER WITHIN THEMSELVES THAT NEEDS TO BE LET OUT. SOMETIMES THEY JUST NEED A LITTLE NUDGE, A LITTLE DIRECTION, A LITTLE SUPPORT, A LITTLE COACHING, AND THE GREATEST THINGS CAN HAPPEN."
- PETE CARROLL

In fact, if you talk with a like-minded person you will likely begin to view it as a goal versus a dream. Many people mentally think that goals are attainable and dreams are fantasies.

However you choose to categorize it, simply knowing that others that can relate to you are in your corner will give you the momentum needed to strive for success.

The overall point here is to simply surround yourself with compatible people who are either on your level or a few steps ahead of where you desire to advance.

"THE BEST WAY A MENTOR CAN PREPARE
ANOTHER LEADER IS TO EXPOSE HIM OR
HER TO OTHER GREAT PEOPLE."
- JOHN C. MAXWELL

It is a great idea at this juncture to find a mentor who has already accomplished the goals that you are seeking to master. Many successful people are very transparent when it comes to sharing the steps they took to arrive at their level of success and would perhaps even be flattered if you would humbly approach them to seek guidance and clarity on your career goals.

However, be careful and perform your due diligence prior to seeking feedback and assistance from a mentor. People help people they like and people who they see trying to help themselves.

"TELL ME AND I FORGET, TEACH ME AND I MAY REMEMBER, INVOLVE ME AND I LEARN."
- BENJAMIN FRANKLIN

You should not under any circumstance expect your mentor to do all of the work, think for you or become your life coach.

Remember, your sole purpose of seeking a mentor is to learn from the best and that is the capacity in which a mentor should be utilized. Always be respectful of their time and remember that they are doing you a favor because they chose to, not because they are required to!

"INSPIRATION IS A TOOL AND A TRAP. IF YOU'RE GOING TO BE INSPIRED BY ANYONE, BE INSPIRED BY PEOPLE WHO HAVE BEEN EXACTLY WHERE YOU ARE NOW."
- DOUGLAS COPELAND

Additionally, it is not uncommon to have more than one mentor, in fact, I suggest that you have a few mentors.

Individuals are typically a subject matter expect (SME) in a particular area. For instance, one of your mentors may have great leadership skills but may not be so great in their execution skills.

"WHAT I'VE FOUND ABOUT IT IS THAT THERE ARE SOME FOLKS YOU CAN TALK TO UNTIL YOU'RE BLUE IN THE FACE--THEY'RE NEVER GOING TO GET IT AND THEY'RE NEVER GOING TO CHANGE. BUT EVERY ONCE IN A WHILE, YOU'LL RUN INTO SOMEONE WHO IS EAGER TO LISTEN, EAGER TO LEARN, AND WILLING TO TRY NEW THINGS. THOSE ARE THE PEOPLE WE NEED TO REACH…." - TYLER PERRY

Remember, it is imperative to seek out people that are at the top of their game. It is better to have a mentor who knows their industry inside and out rather than to have a jack of all trades and a master of none.

It is important to remember that most mentors become lifelong friends. Someone you can consider your maven or go to person during times when you need to make important career decisions but feel uncertain about the choice you should make and how it will impact your life and future endeavors.

"NEVER GIVE UP, FOR THAT IS JUST THE PLACE AND TIME THAT THE TIDE WILL TURN." - HARRIET BEECHER STOWE

A great mentor will recognize your talent, push you past your level of comfort and provide constructive criticism; all of which will inevitably make you better at your craft!

"LIFE IS NOT EASY FOR ANY OF US. BUT WHAT OF THAT? WE MUST HAVE PERSEVERANCE AND ABOVE ALL CONFIDENCE IN OURSELVES. WE MUST BELIEVE THAT WE ARE GIFTED FOR SOMETHING AND THAT THIS THING MUST BE ATTAINED." - MARIE CURIE

"I DO NOT THINK THAT THERE IS ANY
OTHER QUALITY SO ESSENTIAL TO SUCCESS
OF ANY KIND AS THE QUALITY OF
PERSEVERANCE. IT OVERCOMES ALMOST
EVERYTHING, EVEN NATURE."
- JOHN D. ROCKEFELLER

Step # 3

Finding Your 'WHY'

"YOUR PURPOSE IN LIFE IS TO FIND YOUR
PURPOSE AND GIVE YOUR WHOLE HEART
AND SOUL TO IT"
- GAUTAMA BUDDHA

By now you should be in the habit of starting each day with reflection, meditation or prayer. This gives you the opportunity to put on your protective shield before stepping foot outside your fort.

Oftentimes, life throws you a curve ball knowing that it is almost impossible for you to hit it. These are the times your mindset and faith will have to carry you through the storm and to the point of less turbulence.

It is a given that we should always hope for and expect the best but be wise enough to prepare for the worst.

"WHEN THERE ARE THOUGHTS, IT IS DISTRACTION: WHEN THERE ARE NO THOUGHTS, IT IS MEDITATION."
- RAMANA MAHARSHI

A great example of this is a traditional boxing match. If someone were to sucker punch you and you did not see it coming you will likely either be knocked off balance or totally knocked out. It is almost impossible to fully bounce back quickly because the sudden unforeseen action will leave you disoriented and possibility distorted.

"IT'S LESS ABOUT THE PHYSICAL TRAINING, IN THE END, THAN IT IS ABOUT THE MENTAL PREPARATION: BOXING IS A CHESS GAME. YOU HAVE TO BE SKILLED ENOUGH AND HAVE TRAINED HARD ENOUGH TO KNOW HOW MANY DIFFERENT WAYS YOU CAN COUNTERATTACK IN ANY SITUATION, AT ANY MOMENT." -
- JIMMY SMITS

However, if you prepared for every known scenario of the match and stood firm in your stance or ducked upon the punch being thrown at you, you would have the time or tools needed to prepare and brace yourself for the impact.

This boxing match example is just like life. Again, expect the superlative in life but also be prepared for the turmoil.

"YOU HAVE TO RELY ON YOUR PREPARATION. YOU GOT TO REALLY BE PASSIONATE AND TRY TO PREPARE MORE THAN ANYONE ELSE, AND PUT YOURSELF IN A POSITION TO SUCCEED, AND WHEN THE MOMENT COMES YOU GOT TO ENJOY, RELAX, BREATHE AND RELY ON YOUR PREPARATION SO THAT YOU CAN PERFORM AND NOT BE ANXIOUS OR FILLED WITH DOUBT." - STEVE NASH

Step three is a little less challenging than the prior two steps. During step three your sole assignment is to find your 'WHY'. This is the moment that we determine if your success is sustainable.

If your 'WHY' is strong enough, you are guaranteed to be successful, in fact, failure IS NOT an option.

You may ask, "What is my 'WHY' and how do I find it?"

"I FEEL THAT LUCK IS PREPARATION
MEETING OPPORTUNITY."
- OPRAH WINFREY

Your 'WHY' is the reason you wake up, the reason you drag yourself out of bed and for many the reason they go to a job that they totally despise. For some it may be their kids, for others it may be their spouse, their parents or other family members.

The bottom-line is that your 'WHY' will cause you to do things that you dislike but you know that you must do. Your true why makes you totally selfless, makes you realize it is the reason you were put on this earth, and your 'WHY' is commonly your reason for living.

"HE WHO HAS A WHY TO LIVE FOR CAN BEAR ALMOST ANY HOW."
- FRIEDRICH NIETZSCHE

For instance, if I offered you fifty dollars to walk across a ten inch wide by forty foot long wooden plank laying on the floor in front of you, would you do it? Most likely offering someone fifty dollars to walk across a room on solid ground is no challenge and easy money. Personally, I would definitely take that challenge without hesitancy if the opportunity presented itself to me.

"THE PURPOSE OF LIFE IS A LIFE OF PURPOSE."
- ROBERT BRYNE

Now, think about if you were offered that same fifty dollars to walk the same ten inch by forty foot plank but this time is was bridged between two buildings, in fact one hundred story buildings. Would you take the challenge?

If you answered ABSOLUTELY NOT, then you are not alone! The question then becomes, why not? Well it is simple, the risk or your reason.....your 'WHY' changed.

Let us add one more layer to the challenge. What if you were offered the same fifty dollars, to walk the same ten inch by forty foot wooden plank wedged between the same two buildings, still one hundred story each but this

"HAPPINESS DEPENDS UPON OURSELVES."
- ARISTOTLE

time you heard people shouting and quickly realized that those where your children, parents or other family members screaming and the building that they were on top of was engulfed in flames and the fire was quickly rising.

Once again, I would like to ask you, would you walk the ten inch wide by forty foot long wooden plank wedged between the two buildings? If you shouted YES, without hesitation……..then my friend, you have found your 'WHY'.

"EFFORTS AND COURAGE ARE NOT ENOUGH WITHOUT PURPOSE AND DIRECTION."
- JOHN F. KENNEDY

You will know that it is your 'Why' because you would spring into action without pausing for a moment to protect it.

You would not think about yourself for even a split second; in fact, your one and only goal is to get to your most prized possessions and to ensure that they are safe and out of harm's way.

"YOU AREN'T GOING TO FIND ANYBODY THAT'S GOING TO BE SUCCESSFUL WITHOUT MAKING A SACRIFICE AND WITHOUT PERSEVERANCE." - LOU HOLTZ

"WHENEVER YOU HAVE TAKEN UP WORK
IN HAND, YOU MUST SEE IT TO THE FINISH.
THAT IS THE ULTIMATE SECRET OF
SUCCESS. NEVER, NEVER, NEVER GIVE UP!"
- DADA VASWANI

BRIDGET L CHARLES

Step # 4

The Rough Draft

"DON'T WAIT UNTIL EVERYTHING IS JUST RIGHT. IT WILL NEVER BE PERFECT. THERE WILL ALWAYS BE CHALLENGES, OBSTACLES, AND LESS THAN PERFECT CONDITIONS. SO WHAT? GET STARTED NOW. WITH EACH STEP YOU TAKE, YOU WILL GROW STRONGER AND STRONGER, MORE AND MORE SKILLED, MORE AND MORE SELF-CONFIDENT, AND MORE AND MORE SUCCESSFUL."
- MARK VICTOR HANSEN

Step four is the step that will change your life forever. You wake up excited and wondering how you ever started your day without consistently having time for yourself. At this point, you are probably infatuated with the idea of beginning your day with a renewed mind and soul; reflection, mediation or prayer is now engraved as a must-do list rather than a to-do list.

This morning you have the opportunity of basking in the glory of finding your 'WHY' and you are armed and ready to take action.

"WE ARE HUNGRY FOR MORE; IF WE DO NOT CONSCIOUSLY PURSUE THE MORE, WE CREATE LESS FOR OURSELVES AND MAKE IT MORE DIFFICULT TO EXPERIENCE MORE IN LIFE."
- JUDITH WRIGHT

In fact, you are mostly likely so fired up that nothing or no one can stand in your way. You can smell, feel and breathe success at this point.

You know that not being successful is no longer an option. You tell yourself things like having a plan B is just an excuse to fail, it is just an excuse to come in second place. You remind yourself that second place is just the first loser.

"THERE'S NO REASON TO HAVE A PLAN B BECAUSE IT DISTRACTS FROM PLAN A."
- WILL SMITH

You tell yourself that you have been training for this marathon your entire life and now is the time to run the full course. You are hungry, you are driven and you are ready to take action.

The assignment for today is to take your outline and make it a rough draft. You take those steps from the very first day and you write out your life story, word for word. Do not worry or focus on being politically or grammatically correct.

"EVERY GREAT DREAM BEGINS WITH A DREAMER. ALWAYS REMEMBER, YOU HAVE WITHIN YOU THE STRENGTH, THE PATIENCE, AND THE PASSION TO REACH FOR THE STARS TO CHANGE THE WORLD."
- HARRIET TUBMAN

You modestly write your dreams and aspirations down on paper. Seeing the words will prevent you from being able to hide behind your feelings and force you to see and entertain your dreams.

You know that your dreams can come true, you know that your dreams will come true, you are also smart enough to know that anything worth having is worth working hard for and if it was a very simple process…..then EVERYONE would be successful.

"SUCCESS IS NOT A DESTINATION, BUT THE ROAD THAT YOU'RE ON. BEING SUCCESSFUL MEANS THAT YOU'RE WORKING HARD AND WALKING YOUR WALK EVERY DAY. YOU CAN ONLY LIVE YOUR DREAM BY WORKING HARD TOWARDS IT. THAT'S LIVING YOUR DREAM."
- MARLON WAYANS

It is important to realize that the major difference between successful people and unsuccessful people is that successful people stay the course.

When they fall, they do not stay down, they brush themselves off and keep moving.

"NOTHING IN THIS WORLD CAN TAKE THE PLACE OF PERSISTENCE. TALENT WILL NOT: NOTHING IS MORE COMMON THAN UNSUCCESSFUL MEN WITH TALENT. GENIUS WILL NOT; UNREWARDED GENIUS IS ALMOST A PROVERB. EDUCATION WILL NOT: THE WORLD IS FULL OF EDUCATED DERELICTS. PERSISTENCE AND DETERMINATION ALONE ARE OMNIPOTENT." - CALVIN COOLIDGE

One of my favor speakers, Les Brown, often says that "If I fall down I want to fall on my back because if I can look up then I can get up."

Here you will need to keep this momentum going and listen to several motivational books and speakers. You see many people remain on their high when they have someone constantly in their ear reminding them that they can do it.

"SUCCESS SEEMS TO BE CONNECTED WITH ACTION. SUCCESSFUL PEOPLE KEEP MOVING. THEY MAKE MISTAKES BUT DON'T QUIT."
- CONRAD HILTON

The major difference between those people and you is that you will take immediate action to reach your goals.

After all motivation without a plan is just that....motivation. It feels great but when the hype dwindles down, you are right back where you started from. In the same place on a different day!

"ON ONE HAND, WE KNOW THAT EVERYTHING HAPPENS FOR A REASON, AND THERE ARE NO MISTAKES OR COINCIDENCES. ON THE OTHER HAND, WE LEARN THAT WE CAN NEVER GIVE UP, KNOWING THAT WITH THE RIGHT TOOLS AND ENERGY, WE CAN REVERSE ANY DECREE OR KARMA. SO, WHICH IS IT? LET THE LIGHT DECIDE, OR NEVER GIVE UP? THE ANSWER IS: BOTH." - YEHUDA BERG

"THE THREE ORDINARY THINGS THAT WE
OFTEN DON'T PAY ENOUGH ATTENTION
TO, BUT WHICH I BELIEVE ARE THE
DRIVERS OF ALL SUCCESS, ARE HARD WORK,
PERSEVERANCE, AND BASIC HONESTY."
- AZIM PREMJI

Step # 5

Implementation

"I HAVE BEEN IMPRESSED WITH THE
URGENCY OF DOING. KNOWING IS NOT
ENOUGH; WE MUST APPLY. BEING WILLING
IS NOT ENOUGH; WE MUST DO."
- LEONARDO DA VINCI

At this point, your spiritual journey is really progressing. You are really in tuned with yourself; both body and mind. You are getting better at centering your mind and your focus to concentrate on what is important to you.

Your new found sense of awareness will greatly assist you with your task of the day.

"CHANGE WILL NOT COME IF WE WAIT FOR SOME OTHER PERSON OR SOME OTHER TIME. WE ARE THE ONES WE'VE BEEN WAITING FOR. WE ARE THE CHANGE THAT WE SEEK." – BARACK OBAMA

Today is the day of Implementation - it is time to take action! At this stage, your rough draft will be very detailed oriented.

For instance, if you are not happy with your current position at your job, you will write down the steps needed to move to another positon that will fill your void of happiness.

An example would be, "I am not happy with my current career choice. I feel as if I am not living up to my full potential or my true calling in life.

"HAPPINESS HAS TO DO WITH YOUR MINDSET, NOT WITH OUTSIDE CIRCUMSTANCE." - STEVE MARABOLI

I cannot honestly say that I wake up overjoyed to drive forty five minutes to a job that I feel undervalued in. I wish to become a CEO of my own company and focus on helping others."

"When I help others, I have inner peace and joy that goes beyond understanding. Becoming a CEO requires me to take two classes at my local university to complete my studies. I will call the school and get registered within the next two weeks for the next session."

"ALL OF OUR DREAMS CAN COME TRUE IF WE HAVE THE COURAGE TO PURSUE THEM." - WALT DISNEY

"I will check to see if the school offers internship programs to allow me to gain an advance skill-set and I will also volunteer at my local community center at least five hours per week in the business development center."

"I will begin attending networking events that will allow me to align myself with people in the industry and I will call upon my network to keep me in mind if they see any collaborative opportunities that are available."

"BE THE DREAM." - JOHN CHANEY

The next step will give you the opportunity to forecast your future or speak it into existence by pressing fast forward and saying to yourself: "I am so glad that a year ago, I had a dream of being a CEO."

"I took the necessary steps to achieve this goal and I am so happy that today I am a successful CEO, owning a company that I am beyond passionate about!"

The moral of this story and this exercise is that by speaking your desires into existence you are setting the course to succeed.

"PEACE IS NOT MERELY A DISTANT GOAL
THAT WE SEEK BUT A MEANS BY WHICH WE
ARRIVE AT THAT GOAL. "
- MARTIN LUTHER KING, JR

You believe that you will accomplish your goals because you are finally taking action to have the career you deserve and desire. You feel confident because you know that in addition to working hard toward your dreams, you are also taking the necessary steps to get to the next level. You know that in your current state of mind and with your spiritual beliefs, you are destined for greatness, success, joy and inner peace.

"SOME PEOPLE DREAM OF SUCCESS, WHILE OTHER PEOPLE GET UP EVERY MORNING AND MAKE IT HAPPEN."
- WAYNE HUIZENGA

Hopefully, this particular exercise took you from viewing yourself as average to viewing yourself as above average. You look at other business owners and you say to yourself "I know that if they did it, I can definitely do it". You realize that the ONLY thing that separates you from them are opportunity and hard work. You have the hard work down to a science at this point, now you wonder "how can I find the resources and opportunities to finally own my on company?"

"THE TWO MOST IMPORTANT DAYS IN LIFE
ARE THE DAY YOU BORN AND THE DAY
YOU DISCOVER THE REASON WHY."
– MARK TWAIN

At this instant, you have just discovered your AHA moment and you begin to think about all of the connections you have made through your mentors, networking, volunteering and various other resources.

You instantaneously feel excited about your future in the career of your dreams, in other words......you can finally see and feel that your purpose is right at your fingertips.

"I KNOW FROM EXPERIENCE THAT YOU SHOULD NEVER GIVE UP ON YOURSELF OR OTHERS, NO MATTER WHAT."
- GEORGE FOREMAN

"DON'T AIM FOR SUCCESS IF YOU WANT IT;
JUST DO WHAT YOU LOVE AND BELIEVE IN,
AND IT WILL COME NATURALLY."
- DAVID FROST

Step # 6

The Final Draft

"SUCCESS IS A JOURNEY, NOT A
DESTINATION. THE DOING IS OFTEN MORE
IMPORTANT THAN THE OUTCOME."
- ARTHUR ASHE

The final draft…………..the time has come to implement all of the knowledge you have acquired into a central process. You need to eat, breathe and sleep this blueprint presented before you.

Although you can tweak it to match your personality, it is imperative that you not deviate to far from the original blueprint. Compare this success blueprint to a blueprint for a home.

If you change out a few items such as the window designs, the material of the kitchen counter tops or the square footage, you still have the same home.

"ALL YOU NEED IS THE PLAN, THE ROAD MAP, AND THE COURAGE TO PRESS ON TO YOUR DESTINATION." - EARL NIGHTINGALE

However, if you go as far as to change the floorplan layout, the style of home and all of the materials used to build the home, then you have a completely different house which no longer represents the original blueprint.

So again, make this system your own by adding your personal touch but do not go completely off course by implementing extreme changes all at once. By now, you can see clearly into the future, in fact, the future is now intermingle with the present. You wonder to yourself what took me so long to take action and step out on faith?

"FAITH IS TAKING THE FIRST STEP EVEN WHEN YOU DON'T SEE THE WHOLE STAIRCASE." - MARTIN LUTHER KING, JR.

"SUCCESS IS NOT FINAL, FAILURE IS NOT
FATAL: IT IS THE COURAGE TO CONTINUE
THAT COUNTS." - WINSTON CHURCHILL

BRIDGET L CHARLES

Step # 7

Maintenance Zone

"EVERY PERSON WHO WINS IN ANY
UNDERTAKING MUST BE WILLING TO CUT
ALL SOURCES OF RETREAT. ONLY BY DOING
SO CAN ONE BE SURE OF MAINTAINING
THAT STATE OF MIND KNOWN AS A
BURNING DESIRE TO WIN - ESSENTIAL TO
SUCCESS."
- NAPOLEON HILL

Say it with me, YES and YES, I finally got my life on track......I truly took the leap of faith and took possession of my destiny. You have this fabulous new attitude, not only are you motivated but you know how to take action and not simply chase your dreams....but you know how to catch your dreams. In fact, it is no longer your dream but your reality.

You are officially in the maintenance zone. You have found your purpose and you are now living it.

"BELIEVE IN YOURSELF! HAVE FAITH IN YOUR ABILITIES! WITHOUT A HUMBLE BUT REASONABLE CONFIDENCE IN YOUR OWN POWERS YOU CANNOT BE SUCCESSFUL OR HAPPY."
- NORMAN VINCENT PEALE

You have done the most difficult task and now you can ALMOST sit back and enjoy the ride.

The reason I say almost is because continued success requires continuous effort. Maintaining success, inner peace and joy is a life-long journey.

"MAKE TREATING YOURSELF A PRIORITY AND ALWAYS REMEMBER YOUR LIFE IS HAPPENING NOW. DON'T PUT OFF ALL YOUR DREAMS AND PLEASURES TO ANOTHER DAY. IN ANY BALANCED PERSONAL DEFINITION OF SUCCESS THERE HAS TO BE A POWERFUL ELEMENT OF LIVING LIFE IN THE PRESENT."
- MIREILLE GUILIANO

Maintaining Success

Remember to continue to think like a champion and expect success. If you ever become weary, remember the acronym Y.E.S. which for the sake of this exercise means Your Expected Success – you have to have yes in your attitude. Yes should be your ONLY thought! You have to have a yes attitude, an attitude that says…… YES, I know I can do this! Attitude is a choice! Your thoughts definitely dictates your attitude. Therefore you must think positive thoughts in order to keep your mindset in Yes mode.

"SUCCESS COMES FROM TAKING THE INITIATIVE AND FOLLOWING UP…PERSISTING…ELOQUENTLY EXPRESSING THE DEPTH OF YOUR LOVE. WHAT SIMPLE ACTION COULD YOU TAKE TODAY TO PRODUCE A NEW MOMENTUM TOWARD SUCCESS IN YOUR LIFE?"
- TONY ROBBINS

"ALWAYS BE YOURSELF, EXPRESS YOURSELF, HAVE FAITH IN YOURSELF, DO NOT GO OUT AND LOOK FOR A SUCCESSFUL PERSONALITY AND DUPLICATE IT."
- BRUCE LEE

Maintaining Joy

Begin by counting your blessings EVERYDAY! It may help to have a gratitude journal. If you make a daily habit of writing or verbally speaking five things that you are grateful for that also bring you joy, you will quickly realize that joy is often overlooked.

Sometimes we take the small things for granted. Things like having the opportunity to wake up every day, to have your health, to have great family around you. To have the means to feed your family every day.

"THE MORE YOU PRAISE AND CELEBRATE YOUR LIFE, THE MORE THERE IS IN LIFE TO CELEBRATE."
- OPRAH WINFREY

LOL (laugh out loud) is commonly used today when texting, emailing or in general when communicating with people. Perhaps instead of texting or typing it, we should instead practice it!

I am certain that you have heard that laughter is the best medicine. When you laugh, it is nearly impossible to be angry, sad or full of despair. Another step in the process of finding joy is to remove obvious barriers. Perhaps you should consider turning off the news, talk radio and television. Don't worry about missing anything important because unfortunately bad news travel fast.

"GRATITUDE CAN TRANSFORM COMMON DAYS INTO THANKSGIVINGS, TURN ROUTINE JOBS INTO JOY, AND CHANGE ORDINARY OPPORTUNITIES INTO BLESSINGS."
- WILLIAM ARTHUR WARD

I especially feel joy when I listen to inspirational music and watch comedy or feel good movies.

Seek forms of entertainment that uplifts you and steers you toward joy. Another activity that contributes to my joy is volunteering.

I find that when I am giving or assisting others, I do not have the propensity to be depressed or hopeless. It also forces you to be grateful for everything that you have and to not take anything for granted.

"THE INTERIOR JOY WE FEEL WHEN WE
HAVE DONE A GOOD DEED IS THE
NOURISHMENT THE SOUL REQUIRES."
- ALBERT SCHWEITZER

"WHEN YOU DO THINGS FROM YOUR SOUL,
YOU FEEL A RIVER MOVING IN YOU, A JOY."
- RUMI

Maintaining Inner

Peace

Watching other people problems is not a good use of time, needless to say, activities like watching reality television is not your friend.

As a matter of fact, I refer to it as an electronic income reducer (EIR). This is valuable time that you can better allocate by investing in learning something new or enhancing your knowledge and skills. One of my mentors often says, "If it does not make money, it does not make sense." Alternatively, spend that time reading inspirational or educational books, or literature on success and advancement.

"TO ALL THE OTHER DREAMERS OUT THERE, DON'T EVER STOP OR LET THE WORLD'S NEGATIVITY DISENCHANT YOU OR YOUR SPIRIT. IF YOU SURROUND YOURSELF WITH LOVE AND THE RIGHT PEOPLE, ANYTHING IS POSSIBLE."
- ADAM GREEN

Correspondingly, as previously mentioned, finding time to meditate also contributes significantly to inner peace. To reiterate, it helps to center both your body and your mind. It allows you to decompress and shut out all the noise around you. It provides clarity beyond measure.

You have to be healthy in all aspects; mind, body and spirit in order to have total inner peace. Moreover, you have to be willing to do for others without measuring. You have to give without the expectation of receiving.

"SUCCESS IS FINDING SATISFACTION IN GIVING A LITTLE MORE THAN YOU TAKE."
- CHRISTOPHER REEVE

"NEVER CONTINUE IN A JOB YOU DON'T ENJOY. IF YOU'RE HAPPY IN WHAT YOU'RE DOING, YOU'LL LIKE YOURSELF, YOU'LL HAVE INNER PEACE. AND IF YOU HAVE THAT, ALONG WITH PHYSICAL HEALTH, YOU WILL HAVE HAD MORE SUCCESS THAN YOU COULD POSSIBLY HAVE IMAGINED."
- JOHNNY CARSON

BRIDGET L CHARLES

After Thoughts

It is my belief that the combination of success, joy and inner peace is the formula to an abundant life. I sincerely hope that this book provide you with the road map that you need to propel you to the next level. It will take some longer than others to realize that everything that we need to be truly content is either right in front of us or within close proximity.

I encourage you to open your eyes and to not overlook the opportunities presented to you, no matter how small they may seem.

Sometimes a combination of smaller steps lead you to your destination faster than a drastic leap. I encourage you to take time to smell the roses, enjoy your family and be grateful for things that you have while working for the things that you desire.

Remember that although it is important to see and reach the finish line, it is equally important to enjoy the journey.

Just as Oprah Winfrey reminds us, "what material success does is provide you with the ability to concentrate on other things that really matter. And that is being able to make a difference, not only in your own life, but in other people's lives."

Wishing you much Success, Joy & Inner Peace,

Bridget L Charles

"MEMORIES OF OUR LIVES, OF OUR WORKS
AND OUR DEEDS WILL CONTINUE IN
OTHERS." - ROSA PARKS

"AS LONG AS WE ARE PERSISTENCE IN OUR PURSUIT OF OUR DEEPEST DESTINY, WE WILL CONTINUE TO GROW. WE CANNOT CHOOSE THE DAY OR TIME WHEN WE WILL FULLY BLOOM. IT HAPPENS IN ITS OWN TIME." - DENIS WAITLEY

"STAY THE COURSE, LIGHT A STAR, CHANGE
THE WORLD WHERE'ER YOU ARE."
- RICHARD LE GALLIENNE

References

All quotes throughout this book were obtained from www.brainyquote.com and www.goodreads.com. Readers should be advised that the Internet websites listed in this book may have changed or became extinct between the period of time when this book was produced and when it is read.

About the Author

Bridget is a highly sought after author, speaker, business coach, and business development strategist. She is the CEO and founder of Empower Many, a successful company committed to empowering and revitalizing individuals to discover their purpose and excel in their divine purpose in life regardless of the numerous barriers presented in their journey.

Bridget has over 20 years of extensive expertise in corporate training, client acquisition and retention, diversity and inclusion, human resource management, performance management, business development, strategic planning and implementation, ITIL foundations, project management, non-profit management and consulting. Bridget is the embodiment of what Empower Many represents. She has spent the last 10 years helping countless individuals overcome the challenges of being stuck and confused both inside and outside of Corporate America.

She believes that motivation alone is not enough to be successful and that a strategic action plan is also required. She provides the road map needed to assist her clients in their chosen paths – so that they are not only motivated but also have the necessary tools to take action and succeed in their endeavors.

For more information on Bridget, visit:
http://www.bridgetcharles.com

Special

Bonus

Section

A Work in Progress

Just as the title of this book indicates, the goal is to go from being motivated to activated. It is important that you continue to take action daily. Successful people are always working on ways to improve themselves and improve their processes. The steps to success, joy and inner peace are life-long practices and a continuous journey. Additionally, I strongly suggest that you create an annual vision board to assist you in your journey to success. Keep your vision board in plain sight so that it is one of the first things you see when you awake in the morning. Take a picture and make it your screensaver or wallpaper on your computer or your electronic devices. You will be surprised how this constant reminder becomes engraved in your memory, consequently making working toward your goals second nature.

For your convenience, I have included several pages for your notes, reminders, action items or for those golden nuggets also known as AHA moments that will ultimately lead to your personal growth. Additionally, I have included a bonus journal section. Please take these pages and begin to journal your journey. When you put your thoughts, dreams and goals into writing, you have a greater chance of implementing those strategies. This book was designed to be compact enough to allow you the opportunity to take it with you everywhere you go. Use it as you would a mirror to view yourself at all walks of your life. I feel confident that you will look back and view your notes and journal and see your growth over time.

If you would like to drop me a line and share your story or simply provide feedback, I would be delighted. Again, here is to your success. Now - go and share your greatness with the world!

Notes and Reminders

Notes and Reminders

Notes and Reminders

Notes and Reminders

BRIDGET L CHARLES

Notes and Reminders

Notes and Reminders

Notes and Reminders

Notes and Reminders

Notes and Reminders

Notes and Reminders

BRIDGET L CHARLES

Notes and Reminders

Your Journey and Journal Starts Here

BRIDGET L CHARLES

Journal of your Journey

Journal of your Journey

BRIDGET L CHARLES

Journal of your Journey

Journal of your Journey

BRIDGET L CHARLES

Journal of your Journey

Journal of your Journey

BRIDGET L CHARLES

Journal of your Journey

Journal of your Journey

BRIDGET L CHARLES

Journal of your Journey

Journal of your Journey

Journal of your Journey

Journal of your Journey

BRIDGET L CHARLES

Journal of your Journey

Journal of your Journey

BRIDGET L CHARLES

Journal of your Journey

Journal of your Journey

BRIDGET L CHARLES

Journal of your Journey

Journal of your Journey

BRIDGET L CHARLES

Journal of your Journey

Journal of your Journey

BRIDGET L CHARLES

Journal of your Journey

Journal of your Journey

BRIDGET L CHARLES

Journal of your Journey

Journal of your Journey

Journal of your Journey

Journal of your Journey

BRIDGET L CHARLES

Journal of your Journey

Journal of your Journey

BRIDGET L CHARLES

Journal of your Journey

Journal of your Journey

BRIDGET L CHARLES

Journal of your Journey

Journal of your Journey

BRIDGET L CHARLES

Journal of your Journey

Journal of your Journey

Journal of your Journey

MOTIVATED TO ACTIVATED

Journal of your Journey

BRIDGET L CHARLES

Journal of your Journey

Journal of your Journey

BRIDGET L CHARLES

Journal of your Journey

Journal of your Journey

BRIDGET L CHARLES

Journal of your Journey

Journal of your Journey

BRIDGET L CHARLES

Journal of your Journey

Journal of your Journey

BRIDGET L CHARLES

Journal of your Journey

MOTIVATED TO ACTIVATED

Journal of your Journey

BRIDGET L CHARLES

Journal of your Journey

Journal of your Journey

BRIDGET L CHARLES

Journal of your Journey

Journal of your Journey

BRIDGET L CHARLES

Journal of your Journey

Journal of your Journey

BRIDGET L CHARLES

Journal of your Journey

Journal of your Journey

BRIDGET L CHARLES

Journal of your Journey

Journal of your Journey

BRIDGET L CHARLES

Journal of your Journey

Journal of your Journey

BRIDGET L CHARLES

Journal of your Journey

Journal of your Journey

BRIDGET L CHARLES

Journal of your Journey

Journal of your Journey

Journal of your Journey

Journal of your Journey

BRIDGET L CHARLES

Journal of your Journey

Journal of your Journey

BRIDGET L CHARLES

Journal of your Journey

Journal of your Journey

Journal of your Journey

Journal of your Journey

BRIDGET L CHARLES

Journal of your Journey